how2become

ROYAL NAVY RECRUIT TEST
QUESTIONS

by Richard McMunn

Orders: Please contact How2become Ltd, Suite 2, 50 Churchill Square Business Centre, Kings Hill, Kent ME19 4YU.

You can order through Amazon.co.uk under ISBN 9781910202203, via the website www.How2Become.com or through Gardners.com.

ISBN: 9781910202203

First published 2014

Typeset for How2become Ltd by Anton Pshinka.

Printed in Great Britain for How2become Ltd by Bell & Bain Ltd, 303 Burnfield Road, Thornliebank, Glasgow G46 7UQ.

CONTENT

INTRODUCTION

Dear Sir/Madam,

Welcome to your new guide, Royal Navy Recruit Tests: Practice Tests for the Royal Navy selection process for Ratings. This guide contains over 100 pages of sample test questions that are appropriate for anyone who is applying to join the Royal Navy as a Rating.

The selection tests for Armed Forces are designed to assess potential employees 'suitability' for specific posts. In the majority of cases, the higher scores you achieve, the more job opportunities you will have at your disposal. The key to success is to try your hardest to get 100% correct answers in the test that you are undertaking. If you aim for 100% in your preparation, then you are far more likely to achieve the trade or career that you want. We have deliberately supplied you with lots of sample questions to assist you. It is crucial that when you get a question wrong, you take the time to find out why you got it wrong. Understanding the question is very important.

Finally, we recommend that you obtain additional test questions for joining the Royal Navy via our website www.how2become.com. From this website you will be able to find our highly recommended ARMED FORCES TESTS book, which contains a further 250 pages worth of sample test questions to assist you. You will find that the more practice you undertake in the build up to the real test, the better you will perform on the day.

Good luck and best wishes,

The how2become team

The How2become team

PREFACE BY AUTHOR RICHARD MCMUNN

It's probably important that I start off by explaining a little bit about myself, my background, and also why I'm suitably qualified to help you pass the selection tests that form part of the Armed Forces.

At the time of writing I am 42 years old and live in Tunbridge Wells, Kent. I left school at the usual age of 16 and joined the Royal Navy, serving on-board HMS Invincible as part of 800 Naval Air Squadron which formed part of the Fleet Air Arm at the time. There I was at the age of 16, travelling the world and working as an engineer on Sea Harrier jets! It was fantastic and I loved every minute of it. After four years I left the Royal Navy and joined Kent Fire and Rescue Service as a firefighter. Over the next 17 years I worked my way up through the ranks to the position of Assistant Divisional Officer. During my time in the Fire Service I spent a lot of time working as an instructor at the Fire Brigade Training Centre. I was also involved in the selection process for assessing candidates who wanted to join the job as a firefighter. Therefore, my knowledge and experience gained so far in life has been invaluable in helping people like you to pass any type of selection process. I am sure you will find this guide an invaluable resource during your preparation for joining the Armed Forces.

I have always been fortunate in the fact that I persevere at everything I do. I've understand that if I keep working hard in life then I will always be successful; or I will achieve whatever it is that I want to achieve. This is an important lesson that I want you to take on-board straight away. If you work hard and persevere, then success will come your way. The same rule applies whilst applying for a career in the Armed Forces; if you work hard and try lots of test questions, then you will be successful.

Finally, it is very important that you believe in your own abilities. It does not matter if you have no qualifications. It does not matter if you are currently weak in psychometric testing. What does matter is self-belief, self-discipline and a genuine desire to improve and become successful.

Best wishes,

Richard McMunn

Richard McMunn

DISCLAIMER

CHAPTER 1
About the Royal Navy Recruit Test

ABOUT THE ROYAL NAVY RECRUIT TEST

Psychometric tests have been in use in the Armed Forces for many years. They are simply used as a tool to assess a candidates 'ability' to perform specific tasks that are similar to the ones they will have to undertake in a real life scenario. If we break down the word 'psychometric' we can see that 'psycho' means mind and 'metric' means to measure.

Royal Navy Recruit test (RT)

The RT will test your specific academic ability and it is a reflection of how you are likely to perform in a specific role within the Royal Navy. It does not matter what qualifications you have, you will still be required to sit the RT and the results will go towards determining your suitability for the role. How you do on the RT shows your ability to cope with the technical and academic aspects of the Royal Navy training.

Essentially, there are four separate parts of the test which you will need to complete during a strict time limit. These will measure your:

- General reasoning
- Verbal ability
- Numeracy
- Mechanical comprehension

The main purpose of the Royal Navy Recruiting Test is to establish how effective you are at figuring out problems, how good you are at English and Mathematics, and if you can understand basic mechanical concepts. Just like the Army BARB tests, they show the Royal Navy what type of jobs you will most suited to. The Royal Navy Recruiting Test covers the following four areas with time limits:

- A reasoning test (30 questions to be completed in 9 minutes)
- A verbal ability test (30 questions to be completed in 9 minutes)
- A numeracy test (30 questions to be completed in 16 minutes)
- A mechanical reasoning test (30 questions to be completed in 10 minutes)

The tests are usually carried out at the Armed Forces Careers Office and will be under strict timed conditions. Details of the time restrictions and number of questions per exercise will be provided in your recruitment literature. The pass mark for the RN Recruiting Test will very much depend on the technical ability level required for the post you are applying for; although a pass mark of 50% is normally sufficient for the majority of branches.

Now that we have taken the time to understand the types of test that you will be required to sit during the selection process, let's now take a look at some sample test questions for each assessable area.

CHAPTER 2

The Royal Navy Recruit Test – Reasoning Test Questions

THE ROYAL NAVY RECRUIT TEST – REASONING TEST QUESTIONS

During the Royal Navy Recruiting Test you will be required to sit a reasoning test. During the test you will have 9 minutes in which to answer 30 questions. An example of a Royal Navy reasoning test question is as follows:

Sample question number 1

Bill is heavier than Charlie. Who is the lightest?

The answer in this case would be Charlie as the statement indicates that Bill is heavier than Charlie, so therefore Charlie is the lighter of the two.

Answer: Charlie

Here is another example:

Sample question number 2

Graham has more money than Mark. Who is the least wealthy?

The answer in this case would be Mark. The statement indicates that Graham has more money than Mark, therefore implying that Mark has less money.

Answer: Mark

When you are answering this type of question it is important that you READ the question very carefully. The questions are relatively simple but they can catch you out if you do not read them properly. Now take a look at another example:

Sample question number 3

Rubbish is to bin as bread is to?

A. Breadbin

B. Knife

C. Buy

D. Wheat

E. Slice

The answer is A – Breadbin. This is because rubbish goes in the bin and bread goes in the breadbin.

Now try the Royal Navy Recruiting Test sample exercises that are provided over the next few chapters. The time limit for each test is provided at the start of the test.

ROYAL NAVY RECRUIT TEST PRACTICE QUESTIONS - REASONING TEST - EXERCISE 1

During exercise 1 there are 30 sample test questions. Allow yourself 9 minutes to complete the exercise. Once you have finished the exercise, take a look at the answers and see how well you performed.

1. Mark runs twice as long as Stuart.

Who runs for the most amount of time?

Answer

2. Ahmed spends more money at the shop than his friend Bill.

Who spends the least amount of money?

Answer

3. Tony hits his golf shot further than Thomas.

Whose shot travels the least distance?

Answer

4. Car is to drive as aeroplane is to?

Walk

Sail

Fly

Steer

Answer

5. Road is to drive as sea is to?

Swim

Salt

Seaweed

Water

Answer [   ]

6. Fire is to heat as snow is to?

Warm

Melt

White

Freeze

Answer [   ]

7. Happy is the opposite of?

Smile

Sad

Depressed

Upset

Answer [   ]

8. Marcus writes for 3 hours and Stuart writes for 175 minutes

Who writes for the least amount of time?

Answer [   ]

9. Belinda studies for 5 hours and 12 minutes and Sheila studies for 314 minutes.

Who works for the longest period of time?

Answer [   ]

10. Television is to watch as radio is to?

Listen

Hear

Tune

Transmit

Answer [   ]

11. Mountain is to climb as slope is to?

Ice

Fly

Ski

Jump

Answer [   ]

12. Gun is to fire as money is to?

Paper

Coin

Spend

Cash

Answer [   ]

13. Rich is the opposite of?

Poor

Wealthy

Money

Spend

Answer [   ]

14. Untidy means the same as?

Dirty

Messy

Tidy

Wash

Answer [   ]

15. Scared means the same as?

Ghost

Brave

Cry

Afraid

Answer [   ]

16. Co-worker is the same as?

Superior

Colleague

Company

Pupil

Answer

17. Decide is the same as?

Create

Sharp

Resolve

Ensure

Answer

18. Susan swims for 50 minutes whilst Johnathan swims for ¾ of an hour. *Who swims for the least amount of time?*

Answer

19. Billy walks 1100 metres whilst Jenny walks for 1.2 kilometres? *Who walks the furthest?*

Answer

20. Jessica buys two dozen eggs whilst Freya buys 27 eggs.

Who buys the most eggs?

Answer [   ]

21. Ponder is the same as?

Water

Think

Watch

Decide

Answer [   ]

22. Jason watches TV for 79 minutes whilst Andrew watches TV for one hour and thirteen minutes.

Who watches TV for the least amount of time?

Answer [   ]

23. Charlotte runs for 1 mile whilst Jenny runs for 1000 metres?

Who runs the furthest?

Answer [   ]

24. Rodney spends £7.45 at the shops whilst Billy spends 459 pence.

Who spends the least amount of money?

Answer [   ]

25. The red car is twice as fast as the grey car. Which car is slowest?

Answer [   ]

26. Julia is half the weight of her neighbour Jonathan. Who is the heaviest?

Answer [   ]

27. Barry has been playing darts for three times longer than his team mate Paul. Who has played for the least amount of time?

Answer [   ]

28. Jim passed his driving test in 1998 and his wife Gloria passed hers in 1989. Who has held their driving licence the longest?

Answer [   ]

29. Darren lives 13 miles away from his place of work. Jessica's workplace is 12 miles away from her home. Who lives the furthest away from their place of work?

Answer [   ]

30. Rupert has a motorbike which cost £6,450 and Mark has a motorbike which cost £5,654. Who has the least expensive motorbike?

Answer [   ]

ANSWERS TO REASONING EXERCISE 1

1. Mark
2. Bill
3. Thomas
4. Fly
5. Swim
6. Freeze
7. Sad
8. Stuart
9. Sheila
10. Listen
11. Ski
12. Spend
13. Poor
14. Messy
15. Afraid
16. Colleague
17. Resolve
18. Johnathan
19. Jenny
20. Freya
21. Think
22. Andrew
23. Charlotte
24. Billy
25. The grey car
26. Jonathan
27. Paul
28. Gloria
29. Darren
30. Mark

ROYAL NAVY RECRUITING TEST PRACTICE QUESTIONS - REASONING TEST EXERCISE 2

During the Royal Navy Recruiting Test you will find that the reasoning exercise may contain questions in diagrammatic format. Take a look at the following sample question.

Sample question 1

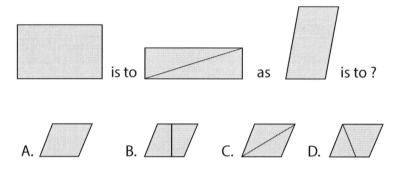

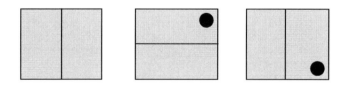

You will notice in the question that the straight line runs diagonally from the bottom left hand corner of the rectangle to the top right hand corner. The rectangle is also smaller in size than its predecessor. Therefore, the correct answer to the question is C, as the straight line runs the same through the shape, and it too is slightly smaller in size.

Take a look at the next question.

Sample question 2

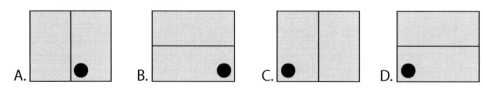

Which of the following shapes comes next in the sequence?

The correct answer is D. You will notice in the sample question that the black dot is moving around the shapes in a clockwise manner. In addition to this the line that runs through the shape is alternating from vertical to horizontal. The black dot starts off in the top left hand corner of the first shape. Then it progresses to the top right hand corner of the second shape before moving round to the bottom right hand corner of the third shape. Therefore D, where the black dot is in the bottom left hand corner of the shape with the horizontal line is the correct answer.

Now try Reasoning Exercise 2 which contains sample diagrammatic test questions. You have 10 minutes in which to answer 20 questions.

ROYAL NAVY RECRUITING TEST PRACTICE QUESTIONS - REASONING TEST EXERCISE 2

Question 1

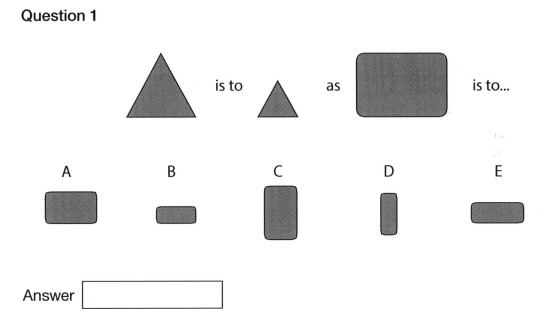

Answer

Question 2

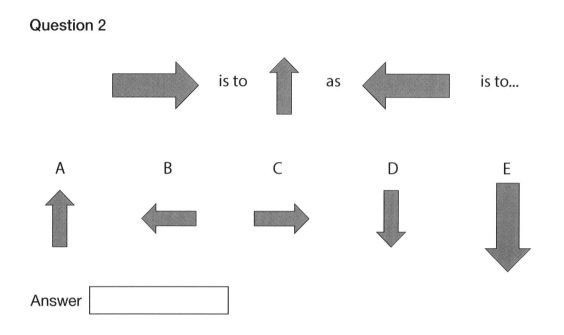

Answer [   ]

Question 3

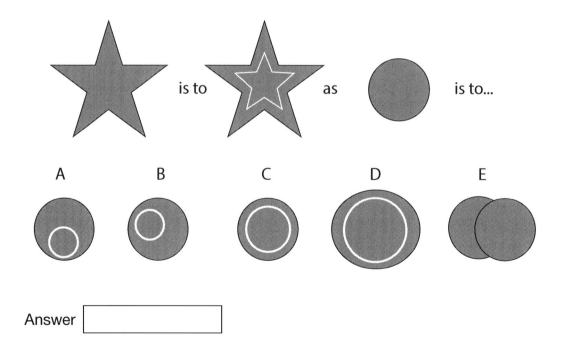

Answer [   ]

Question 4

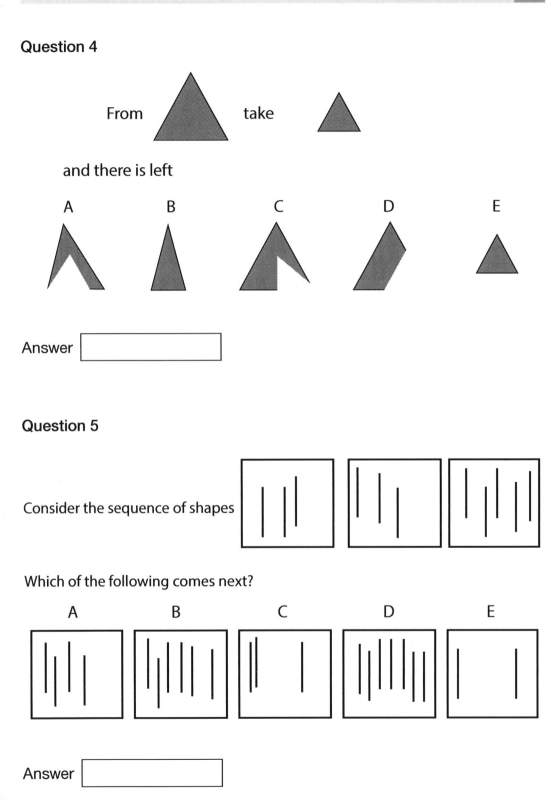

From ▲ take ▲

and there is left

A   B   C   D   E

Answer [   ]

Question 5

Consider the sequence of shapes

Which of the following comes next?

A   B   C   D   E

Answer [   ]

Question 6

Consider the sequence of shapes

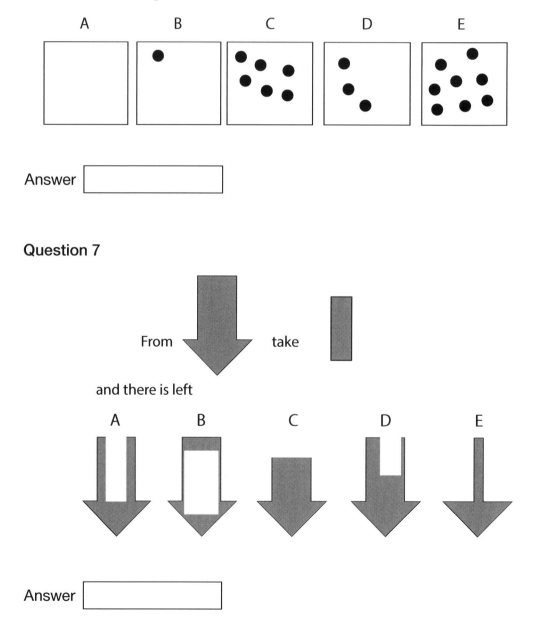

Which of the following comes next?

A   B   C   D   E

Answer

Question 7

From ⬇ take ▮

and there is left

A   B   C   D   E

Answer

Question 8

Consider the sequence of shapes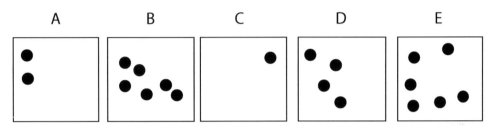

Which of the following comes next?

A   B   C   D   E

Answer [   ]

Question 9

Consider the sequence of shapes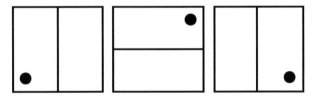

Which of the following comes next ?

A.   B.   C.   D.   E

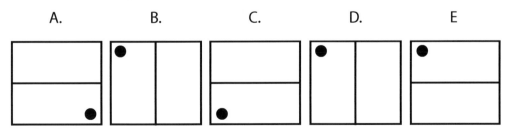

Answer [   ]

Question 10

Consider the following sequence

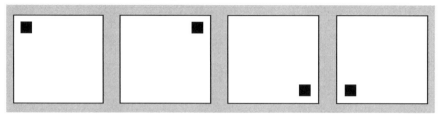

Which of the following comes next?

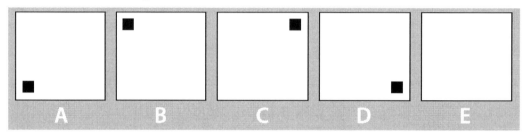

Answer [   ]

Question 11

Consider the following sequence

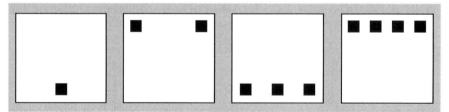

Which of the following comes next?

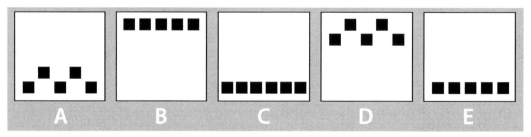

Answer [   ]

Question 12

Consider the following sequence

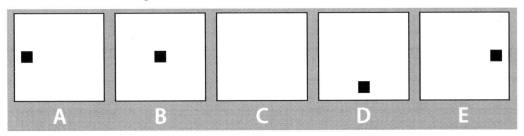

Which of the following comes next?

Answer [   ]

Question 13

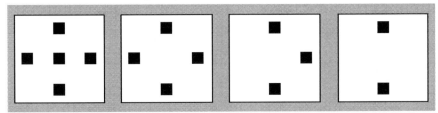

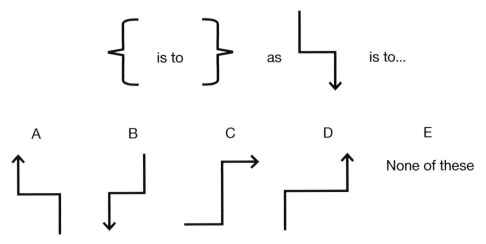

Answer

Question 14

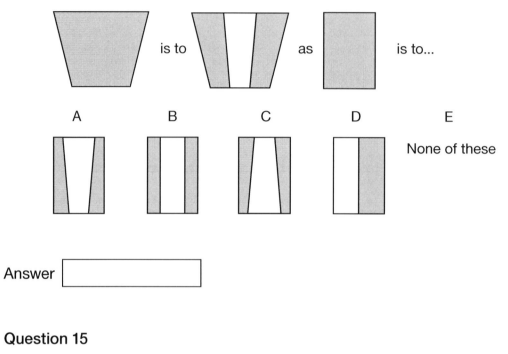

A   B   C   D   E

None of these

Answer

Question 15

Consider the following sequence

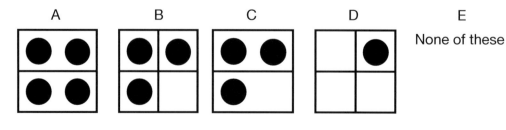

Which of the following comes next?

A   B   C   D   E

None of these

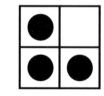

Answer

Question 16

Consider the following sequence

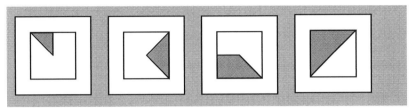

Which of the following comes next?

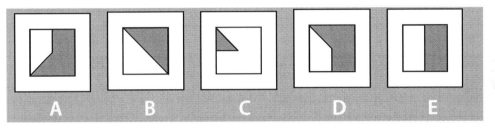

Answer [   ]

Question 17

Consider the following sequence

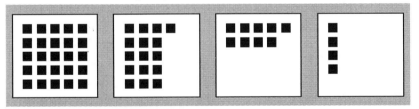

Which of the following comes next?

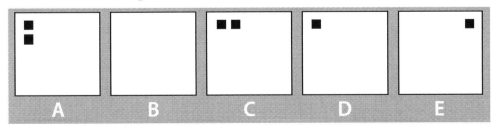

Answer [   ]

Question 18

Consider the sequence of shapes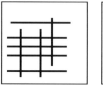

Which of the following comes next?

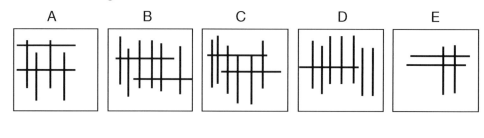

Answer [   ]

Question 19

Two of the diagram options (A and D) are identical. One of them should be a slight variant.

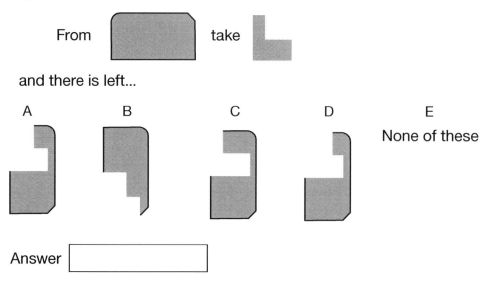

and there is left...

Answer [   ]

Question 20

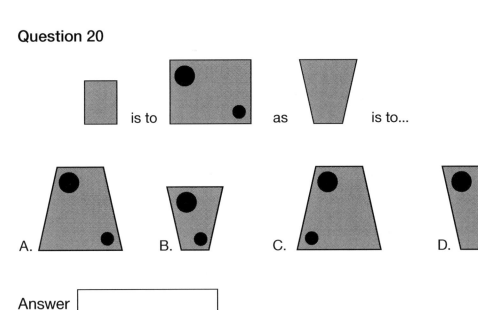

Answer [   ]

Now that you have completed reasoning exercise 2 take the time to work through the answers carefully checking to see which, if any, you got wrong.

ANSWERS TO REASONING EXERCISE 2

1. A

2. D

3. C

4. D

5. B

6. B (the number of black dots within each square is halving as the sequence progresses)

7. A

8. C (the number of black dots within each square is decreasing by 3 each time as the sequence progresses)

9. E

10. B

11. E

12. D

13. B

14. B

15. A

16. D

17. D

18. C (the vertical lines are increasing by 1 each time throughout the sequence and the horizontal lines decreasing by 1)

19. C

20. D

ROYAL NAVY RECRUITING TEST PRACTICE QUESTIONS - REASONING TEST EXERCISE 3

During the Royal Navy Recruiting Test you will find that the reasoning exercise may contain questions in numerical format. Take a look at the following sample question.

Sample question 1

Take a look at the following row of numbers. Which number comes next from the options available?

2, 8, 14, 20, 26, 32, ?

A. 64   B. 38   C. 39   D. 42   E. 54

The answer is B – 38. The numbers are rising by 6 each time.

Now take a look at the next sample question.

Sample question 2

Take a look at the following row of numbers. Which number represents '?' from the options available?

2, 2, 4, 4, 16, 6, 256, ?

A. 8   B. 512   C. 250   D. 12   E. 24

The answer is A – 8. The 1st, 3rd and 5th numbers in the row are multiples of each other. For example, 2 x 2 = 4, 4 x 4 = 16, 16 x 16 = 256. The 2nd, 4th and 6th numbers are all increasing by 2 each time. Therefore, the 8th number in the sequence will be 8.

Once you understand what is required in the test move onto the following exercise. There are 20 questions and you have a total of 7 minutes in which to answer them.

ROYAL NAVY RECRUITING TEST PRACTICE QUESTIONS - REASONING TEST EXERCISE 3

Question 1

Take a look at the following row of numbers. Which number represents '?' from the option available?

1, 3, 5, ?, 9

A. 11   B. 6   C. 7   D. 9   E. 8

Answer

Question 2

Take a look at the following row of numbers. Which number represents '?' from the options available?

10, 14, 11, 15, ?, 16, 13, 17

A. 11   B. 12   C. 13   D. 14   E. 15

Answer

Question 3

Take a look at the following row of numbers. Which number represents '?' from the options available?

11, 16, ?, 26, 31, 36, 41

A. 18   B. 19   C. 20   D. 21   E. 23

Answer [   ]

Question 4

Take a look at the following row of numbers. Which number comes next from the options available?

5, 5, 15, 10, 25, 15, 35, ?

A. 20   B. 25   C. 30   D. 35   E. 40

Answer [   ]

Question 5

Take a look at the following row of numbers. Which number comes next from the options available?

110, 14, 104, 15, 98, 16, ?

A. 92   B. 17   C. 90   D. 111   E. 90

Answer [   ]

Question 6

Take a look at the following row of numbers. Which number comes next from the options available?

76, 2, 64, 8, ?, 14, 40, 20, 28

A. 50   B. 52   C. 16   D. 42   E. 20

Answer [   ]

Question 7

Take a look at the following row of numbers. Which number comes next from the options available?

44, 20, 40, 24, 36, 28, 32, 32, ?

A. 28   B. 24   C. 36   D. 34   E. 44

Answer [   ]

Question 8

Take a look at the following row of numbers. Which number represents '?' from the options available?

25, 50, 100, 200, 400, 800, ?

A. 200   B. 400   C. 160   D. 2400   E. 1600

Answer [   ]

Question 9

Take a look at the following row of numbers. Which number comes next from the options available?

3, 56, 5, 50, 7, 42, 9, 32, 11, ?

A. 14   B. 22   C. 16   D. 18   E. 20

Answer

Question 10

Take a look at the following row of numbers. Which number comes next from the options available?

2, 5, 4, 8, 8, 14, 16, 23, 32, ?

A. 40   B. 32   C. 35   D. 36   E. 34

Answer

Question 11

Take a look at the following row of numbers. Which number comes next from the options available?

10, 5, 8, 6, 6, 7, 4, ?

A. 0   B. 2   C. 8   D. 9   E. 12

Answer

Question 12

Take a look at the following row of numbers. Which two numbers in order of sequence represent '?' from the options available?

?, 115, 100, 85, 70, ?

A. 145 and 60   B. 130 and 55   C. 100 and 60   D. 110 and 100   E. 150 and 35

Answer [   ]

Question 13

Take a look at the following row of numbers. Which two numbers in order of sequence represent '?' from the options available?

?, 46, 37, 29, 22, 16, ?

A. 56 and 11   B. 53 and 10   C. 48 and 12   D. 38 and 14   E. 55 and 9

Answer [   ]

Question 14

Take a look at the following row of numbers. Which two numbers in order of sequence represent '?' from the options available?

1, ?, 15, 22, ?, 36, 43

A. 7 and 28   B. 5 and 30   C. 9 and 28   D. 10 and 36   E. 8 and 29

Answer [   ]

Question 15

Take a look at the following row of numbers. Which two numbers in order of sequence represent '?' from the options available?

?, 178, 152, 126, ?, 74, 48, 22

A. 212 and 104   B. 204 and 100   C. 200 and 86   D. 234 and 98   E. 196 and 80

Answer [   ]

Question 16

Take a look at the following row of numbers. Which two numbers in order of sequence represent '?' from the options available?

34, 45, ?, 67, ?, 89

A. 56 and 78   B. 55 and 70   C. 52 and 80   D. 49 and 72   E. 45 and 71

Answer [   ]

Question 17

Take a look at the following row of numbers. Which two numbers in order of sequence represent '?' from the options available?

66, 31, 57, 40, 48, 49, 39, ?, ?

A. 56 and 20   B. 44 and 32   C. 49 and 31   D. 58 and 30   E. 50 and 33

Answer [   ]

Question 18

Take a look at the following row of numbers. Which number comes next from the options available?

3, 9, ?, 81, 243, 729, 2187

A. 44   B. 27   C. 18   D. 59   E. 32

Answer [   ]

Question 19

Take a look at the following row of numbers. Which number comes next from the options available?

10001, 9989, 9965, ?, 9821, 9629

A. 9944   B. 9917   C. 9729   D. 9894   E. 9921

Answer [   ]

Question 20

Take a look at the following row of numbers. Which number comes next from the options available?

64, 66, 70, 76, 84, ?

A. 86   B. 88   C. 92   D. 90   E. 94

Answer [   ]

Now that you've completed exercise 3, work through your answers carefully checking to see which, if any, you got wrong.

ANSWERS TO REASONING EXERCISE 3

1. C- The sequence is rising by 2 each time.

2. B – Each number increases by 1 more each time. E.g. 9+1=10, 10+2=12, 12+3=15, 15+4=19 etc.

3. D – Each number increases by 10.

4. A – All odd numbers are increasing by 5 each time and all even numbers are increasing by 10.

5. A – All the odd numbers are decreasing by 6 each time and all the even numbers are increasing by 1.

6. B – All odd numbers are decreasing by 12 and all even numbers are increasing by 6.

7. A – The sequence is decreasing by 4 each time whilst the other run of numbers increase by 4 each time

8. E – All numbers are increasing by multiples of 2 each time. For example: 25x2=50, 50x2=100, 100x2=200 etc.

9. E – The odd numbers are increasing by 2 each time. The even numbers decrease as follows:

$56 - 6 = 50, 50 - 8 = 42, 42 - 10 = 32, 32 - 12 = 20$

You will notice that the number subtracted each time increases by 2.

10. C – Both odd numbers and even numbers are increasing as follows:

Even numbers:

$2 + 2 = 4$

$4 + 4 = 8$

$8 + 8 = 16$

$16 + 16 = 32$

Odd numbers:

$5 + 3 = 8$

8 + 6 = 14

14 + 9 = 23

23 + 12 = 35

You will note that the numbers add each time for both odd and even numbers increases by 3.

11. C – The even numbers are decreasing 2 each time and the odd numbers are increasing by 1.

12. B – The numbers are decreasing by 15 each time.

13. A – The numbers are decreasing as follows:

56 – 10 = 46

46 – 9 = 37

37 – 8 = 29

29 – 7 = 22

22 – 6 = 16

16 – 5 = 11

14. E – The numbers are increasing by 7 each time.

15. B – The numbers are decreasing by 26 each time.

16. A – The numbers are increasing by 11 each time.

17. D – One set of numbers are decreasing by 9 each time and the other set of numbers are increasing by 9 each time.

18. B – Each number is multiplied by 3 each time.

19. B – The numbers are decreasing each time as follows:

For example:

10001 – 12 = 9989

9989 – 24 = 9965

9965 – 48 = 9917

9917 – 96 = 9821

20. E – The numbers are increasing each time as follows:

64 + 2 = 66

66 + 4 = 70

70 + 6 = 76

76 + 8 = 84

84 + 10 = 94

CHAPTER 3

The Royal Navy Recruit Test – Verbal Ability Test Questions

ROYAL NAVY RECRUIT TEST PRACTICE QUESTIONS - VERBAL ABILITY TEST

During this part of the Royal Navy Recruiting test you will be required to answer 30 questions in 9 minutes. This test is designed to assess your English language skills. The test is multiple-choice in nature you will have 5 options to choose from. The most effective way to prepare for this type of test is to practice sample questions under timed conditions. Other ways for improving your ability include carrying out crosswords, word searches or any other tests that require an ability to work with the English language. You may also decide to purchase your own psychometric testing booklet, which can be obtained from the website **www.how2become.com**

Take a look at the following sample question.

Sample question 1

Which of the following words is the odd one out?

A. Hammer   B. Table   C. Chisel   D. Pliers   E. Wrench

The answer is B –Table. This is because all of the other items are tools and the table is an item used for different purposes, therefore the odd one out.

Now take a look at the next sample question.

Sample question 2

The following sentence has one word missing. Which word makes the best sense of the sentence?

He had been ………… for a very long time and was now starting to lose his concentration.

A. moaning   B. irritating   C. driving   D. making   E. meeting

The correct answer is C – driving, as this word makes best sense of the sentence.

Now try the following verbal ability exercise. There are 30 questions and you have 9 minutes in which to complete them.

ROYAL NAVY RECRUITING TEST PRACTICE QUESTIONS VERBAL ABILITY TEST – EXERCISE 1

Question 1

Which of the following words is the odd one out?

A. Desk   B. Shelf   C. Cupboard   D. Chair   E. Wood

Answer [   ]

Question 2

Which of the following is the odd one out?

A. Eyes   B. Nose   C. Finger   D. Lips   E. Ear

Answer [   ]

Question 3

The following sentence has one word missing. Which word makes the best sense of the sentence?

He found the walk to work each day ……….

A. Healthy   B. Happy   C. Funny   D. Car   E. Wet

Answer [   ]

Question 4

The following sentence has two words missing. Which two words make best sense of the sentence?

The man _____ his jog at 6am and was _____ home at 7am

A. started / really

B. left / finally

C. wanted / left

D. began / back

E. originated / once

Answer

Question 5

In the line below, the word outside of the brackets will only go with three of the words inside the brackets to make longer words. Which ONE word will it NOT go with?

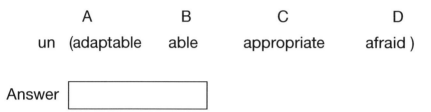

	A	B	C	D
un	(adaptable	able	appropriate	afraid)

Answer

Question 6

In the line below, the word outside of the brackets will only go with three of the words inside the brackets to make longer words. Which ONE word will it NOT go with?

	A	B	C	D
un	(affected	alike	adjusted	capable)

Answer

Question 7

In the line below, the word outside of the brackets will only go with three of the words inside the brackets to make longer words. Which ONE word will it NOT go with?

	A	B	C	D
In	(censing	stoppable	diction	draught)

Answer [   ]

Question 8

Which of the following words is the odd one out?

A.Gold   B. Titanium   C. Iron   D. Ivory   E. Silver

Answer [   ]

Question 9

Which of the following words is the odd one out?

A.Sword   B. Dagger   C. Arrow   D. Spear   E. Shield

Answer [   ]

Question 10

Which of the following words is the odd one out?

A.Bird   B. Dog   C. Helicopter   D. Plane   E. Cloud

Answer [   ]

Question 11

Which of the following words is the odd one out?

A.Jupiter   B. Earth   C. Mars   D. Moon   E. Saturn

Answer [   ]

Question 12

Which of the following is the odd one out?

A.Biscuit   B. Tea   C. Milk   D. Coffee   E. Water

Answer [   ]

Question 13

The following sentence has one word missing. Which word makes the best sense of the sentence?

He brought a guitar as a gift and _____ it to his dad.

A. Received   B. Given   C. Ran   D. Threw   E. Gave

Answer [   ]

Question 14

Which two letter word can be placed in front of the following words to make a new word?

Setting   Strokes   Visibly   Tuition

Answer [   ]

Question 15

Which five letter word can be placed in front of the following words to make a new word?

Till   Play   View   Zone

Answer [   ]

Question 16

The following sentence has one word missing. Which ONE word makes the best sense of the sentence?

The weather forecaster informed the public of the _____ rain

A. Likelihood   B. Chance   C. Dry   D. Need   E. Potential

Answer [   ]

Question 17

The following sentence has one word missing. Which ONE word makes the best sense of the sentence?

The runner had run 10 _____ today.

A. Days   B. Gallons   C. Miles   D. centimetres   E. Months

Answer [   ]

Question 18

The following sentence has two words missing. Which TWO words make the best sense of the sentence?

A bank is a _____ institution where people deposit their money to keep it _____.

A. business / energetic

B. charity / loose

C. financial / safe

D. processing / increase

E. money / hidden

Answer [   ]

Question 19

The following sentence has one word missing. Which ONE word makes the best sense of the sentence?

A submarine is a watercraft _____ of independent operation underwater.

A. evolved   B. built   C. capable   D. designed   E. submersible

Answer [   ]

Question 20

Which of the following is the odd one out?

A. Trumpet   B. Violin   C. Harp   D. Guitar

Answer [   ]

Question 21

Which of the following is the odd one out?

A. July   B. May   C. June   D. December

Answer [   ]

Question 22

Which of the following is the odd one out?

A. Lake   B. Stream   C. River   D. Water

Answer [   ]

Question 23

Which of the following is the odd one out?

A. House   B. Shed   C. Flat   D. Bungalow

Answer [   ]

Question 24

Which of the following is the odd one out?

A. Pen   B. Crayon   C. Pencil   D. Ink

Answer [   ]

Question 25

Which of the following is the odd one out?

A. Blazer   B. Shorts   C. Shirt   D. Cloth

Answer [   ]

Question 26

The following sentence has one word missing. Which ONE word makes the best sense of the sentence?

The man _____ he wanted to go home.

A. chose   B. needed   C. decided   D. ran   E. boasted

Answer [   ]

Question 27

The following sentence has one word missing. Which ONE word makes the best sense of the sentence?

The man always took his dog for a _____ walk.

A. boring   B. daily   C. funny   D. sudden   E. running

Answer [   ]

Question 28

The following sentence has one word missing. Which ONE word makes the best sense of the sentence?

The woman went swimming _____ work.

A. whilst   B. needing   C. choosing   D. to   E. after

Answer [   ]

Question 29

In the line below, the word outside of the brackets will only go with three of the words inside the brackets to make longer words. Which ONE word will it NOT go with?

	A	B	C	D
Un	(abating	admired	anchors	draught)

Answer [   ]

Question 30

In the line below, the word outside of the brackets will only go with three of the words inside the brackets to make longer words. Which ONE word will it NOT go with?

	A	B	C	D
An	(elastic	aerobic	navy	droid)

Answer [   ]

ANSWERS TO VERBAL ABILITY EXERCISE 1

1. E
2. C
3. A
4. D
5. C
6. D
7. B
8. D
9. E
10. B
11. D
12. A
13. E
14. In
15. Inter
16. E
17. C
18. C
19. C
20. A
21. D
22. D
23. B
24. D
25. D
26. C
27. B
28. E
29. D
30. C

CHAPTER 4

The Royal Navy Recruit Test – Mechanical Comprehension Test Questions

ROYAL NAVY RECRUITING TEST PRACTICE QUESTIONS

MECHANICAL COMPREHENSION TEST

During the Royal Navy Recruiting test you will be required to sit a mechanical comprehension test. Mechanical comprehension tests are an assessment that measures an individual's ability to learn and understand mechanical concepts. The tests are usually multiple-choice in nature and present simple, frequently encountered mechanisms and situations. The majority of mechanical comprehension tests require a working knowledge of basic mechanical operations and the application of physical laws. On the following pages I have provided you with a number of example questions to help you prepare for the tests. Work through them as quickly as possible but remember to go back and check which ones you get wrong; more importantly, make sure you understand how the correct answer is reached.

In this particular exercise there are 20 questions and you have 10 minutes in which to answer them.

ROYAL NAVY RECRUIT TEST MECHANICAL COMPREHENSION TEST 1

Question 1

Which weight requires the most force to lift it?

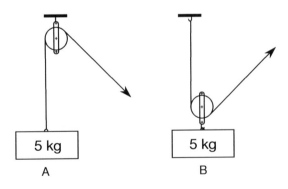

A. Both the same

B. A

C. B

Answer

Question 2

How much weight is required to balance point X?

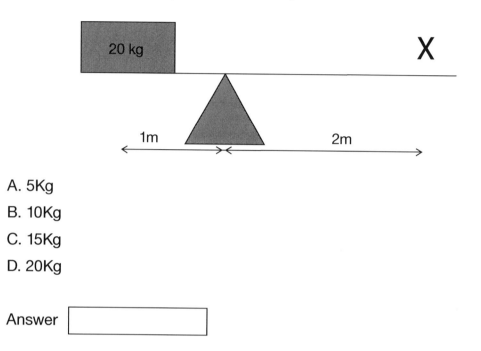

A. 5Kg

B. 10Kg

C. 15Kg

D. 20Kg

Answer [   ]

Question 3

If cog C turns anti-clockwise at a speed of 10rpm, which way and at what speed will cog B turn?

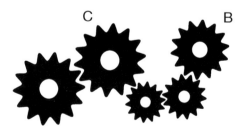

A. 10rpm / anti-clockwise

B. 10rpm / clockwise

C. 20rpm / anti-clockwise

D. 20rpm / clockwise

Answer [   ]

Question 4

Which tool would you use to claw nails from wood?

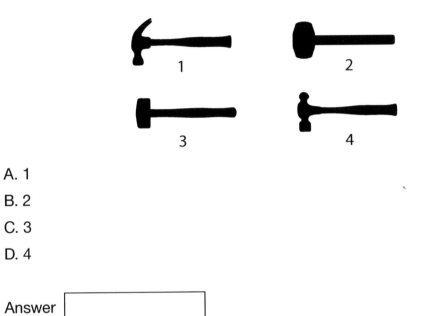

A. 1

B. 2

C. 3

D. 4

Answer [   ]

Question 5

If bulb 2 is removed which bulbs will illuminate?

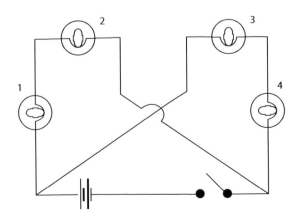

A. 1

B. 3

C. 4

D. None

Answer

Question 6

When the switch is closed how many bulbs will illuminate when bulb 3 is removed?

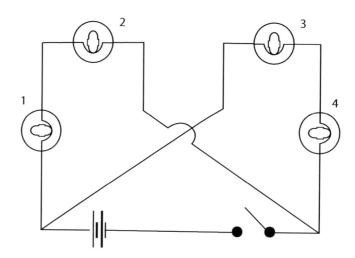

A. None

B. One

C. Two

D. Three

Answer

Question 7

If cog B turns anti-clockwise which way will cog A turn?

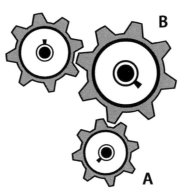

A. Clockwise

B. Anti-clockwise

Answer [   ]

Question 8

If wheel A is three times the diameter of wheel B and it rotates at 55rpm, what speed will wheel B rotate at?

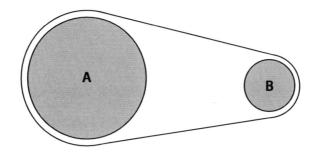

A. 55 rpm

B. 110 rpm

C. 165 rpm

Answer

Question 9

How much force is required to lift the 75 kg weight?

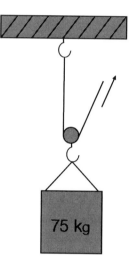

A. 15 kg

B. 32.5 kg

C. 75 kg

D. 150 kg

Answer

Question 10

A screw has 8 threads per inch. How many full turns are required for the nut to travel 3 inches?

A. 8 turns

B. 12 turns

C. 16 turns

D. 24 turns

Answer [   ]

Question 11

Cog A has 12 teeth and Cog B has 18 teeth. If cog B completes two full turns, how many rotations will cog A complete?

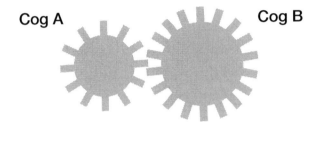

A. 3 rotations

B. 2 rotations

C. 1.5 rotations

D. 1 rotation

Answer [   ]

Question 12

If cog 4 turns anti-clockwise, which other cogs will also turn anti-clockwise?

A. 1 and 2

B. 1 and 3

C. 3 and 4

D. 2 and 3

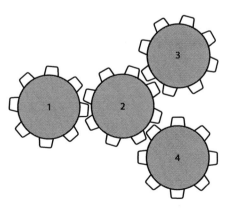

Answer [   ]

Question 13

A thick block of wood rests on an even and level surface. What mechanical principle makes it more difficult to push this block sideways if the surface is made of sandpaper than if it is made of glass?

A. Spring force

B. Gravitational force

C. Air resistance force

D. Frictional force

Answer [   ]

Question 14

When water is poured in to a tank, what happens to the pressure on the surface?

A. Decreases

B. Stays the same

C. Increases

Answer [   ]

Question 15

The following three HGV's are parked on an incline. Their centre of gravity is identified by a dot. Which of the three HGV's is most likely to fall over?

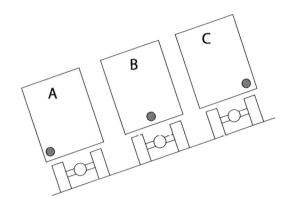

A. A

B. B

C. C

Answer

Question 16

Which of the following most resembles a lever?

A. Swing

B. Car

C. Elevator

D. Seesaw

Answer

Question 17

To balance the beam how much weight should be placed on the right hand side?

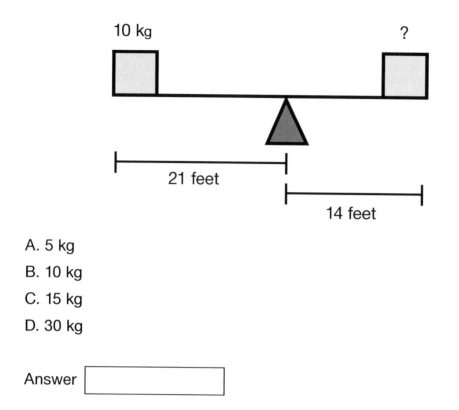

A. 5 kg

B. 10 kg

C. 15 kg

D. 30 kg

Answer [   ]

Question 18

How far from the balance point should the 30 kg weight be placed to balance the beam?

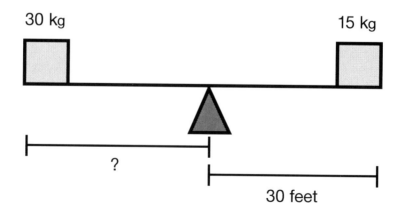

A. 5 feet

B. 10 feet

C. 15 feet

D. 45 feet

Answer [   ]

Question 19

How far would you have to pull the rope up to lift the weight 5 feet?

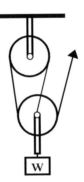

A. 5 feet

B. 10 feet

C. 15 feet

D. 30 feet

Answer [   ]

Question 20

If cog X turns 40 times, how many times will cog Y turn?

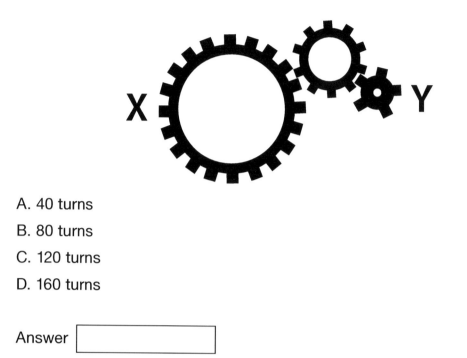

A. 40 turns

B. 80 turns

C. 120 turns

D. 160 turns

Answer [   ]

Now that you have completed mechanical comprehension exercise 1, check your answers carefully before moving onto the exercise 2.

ANSWERS TO MECHANICAL COMPREHENSION TEST 1

1. B

When answering questions where there is a single pulley system if the pulley is fixed, as in A, then the force required to lift the weight is the same as the weight, i.e. 5Kg. However, where the pulley system is not fixed and it moves with the weight, as is the case with pulley system B, then the weight required to lift it is half the weight. This means that the weight required to lift B is 2.5kg. The answer to the questions is therefore B as pulley system A requires the most weight to lift it.

2. B

Point X is twice the distance from the balance point; therefore, half the weight is required. The answer is B, 10Kg.

3. B

If cog C turns 10 anti-clockwise at a speed of 10rpm then it is relatively straight forward to determine that cob B will rotate the same speed but in a clockwise direction.

4. A

The only tool that you can use from the selection to claw nails from wood is claw hammer A.

5. D

No bulbs would illuminate because the circuit, in its current state, is not working. This is due to the switch being open.

6. C

Only two bulbs would illuminate (bulbs 1 and 2). The broken circuit would prevent bulb 4 from illuminating.

7. A

Cog A will turn clockwise.

8. C

Because wheel A is three times greater in diameter than wheel B, each revolution of A will lead to 3 times the revolution of B. Therefore, if wheel A rotates at 55 rpm, B will rotate at 55 rpm × 3 = 165 rpm.

9. B

This type of pulley system has a mechanical advantage of 2. Therefore, to lift the 75 kg weight will require 57 kgs ÷ 2 = 32.5 kgs.

10. D

There are 8 threads per inch. To move the nut 3 inches will require 8 × 3 = 24 turns.

11. A

Each full turn of cog B will result in 18 teeth ÷ 12 teeth = 1.5 rotations. Two turns of cog B will result in cog A completing 3 rotations.

12. B

Cogs 1 and 3 will also turn anti-clockwise. Cog 2 is the only cog which will rotate clockwise.

13. D

In this particular case frictional force is the force that must be overcome in order to slide the object from one side to another.

14. B

The pressure at the surface remains the same, since it has a finite amount of water above it.

15. A

By drawing a vertical line straight down from the centre of gravity, only the line for HGV A reaches the ground outside of its tyres. This makes the HGV unstable.

16. D

A seesaw is the only option which utilises a form of leverage to function.

17. C

The distance of the weight on the right hand side from the balance point is one third less than the distance on the right hand side; therefore, an additional third weight is required to balance the beam.

18. C.

In order to balance the beam the weight needs to be placed half the distance of the right hand side (15 feet). This is because the weight on the left is twice as heavy as the weight on the right hand side.

19. C

You would need to lift the rope 15 feet in order to lift the weight 5 feet.

20. D

Cog X has a total of 20 teeth, whereas cog Y has a total of 5 teeth. Because cog Y has four times fewer teeth than cog X, it will rotate four times for every single full rotation cog X achieves.

MECHANICAL COMPREHENSION TEST 2

Question 1

Which gate is the strongest?

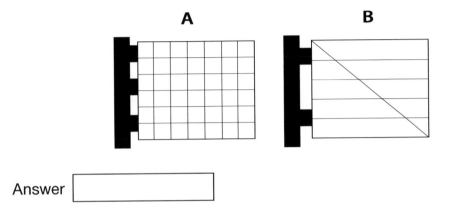

Answer [   ]

Question 2

Which of the following pulley systems has a mechanical advantage of 3?

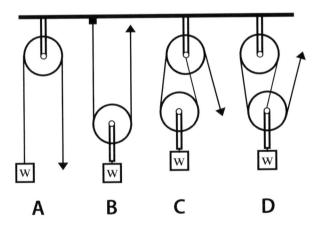

A. A and B

B. C and D

C. B and D

D. D

E. None of them

Answer [   ]

Question 3

Which direction should the wind blow in order for the plane to take off with the shortest runway?

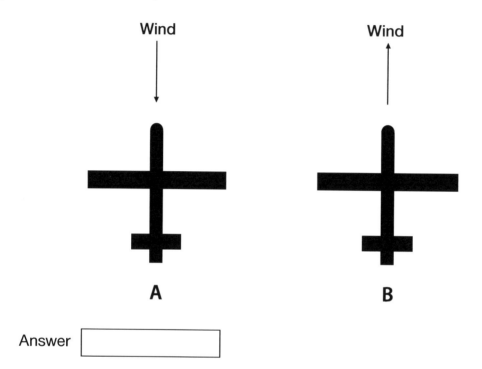

Answer [   ]

Question 4

Which wheel will rotate the least number of times in one hour?

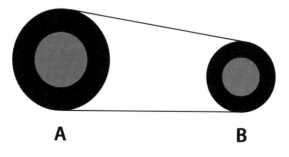

A. Wheel A

B. Wheel B

Answer [   ]

Question 5

If cog Y moves anticlockwise which way will cog X move?

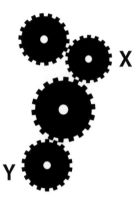

A. Wheel A

B. Wheel B

Answer [   ]

Question 6

If Cog C rotates clockwise at a speed of 120 rpm, at what speed and direction will Cog A rotate? (rpm = revolutions per minute)

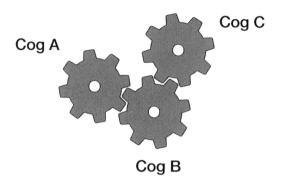

A. 120 rpm clockwise

B. 120 rpm anticlockwise

C. 40 rpm clockwise

D. 40 rpm anticlockwise

Answer [   ]

Question 7

A cannonball is fired from a cannon horizontally. At the same time you drop a cannonball of the same weight from the same height. Which will hit the ground first?

A. Dropped ball

B. Fired ball

C. Both the same

Answer [   ]

Question 8

How much weight in kilograms will need to be added in order to balance the beam?

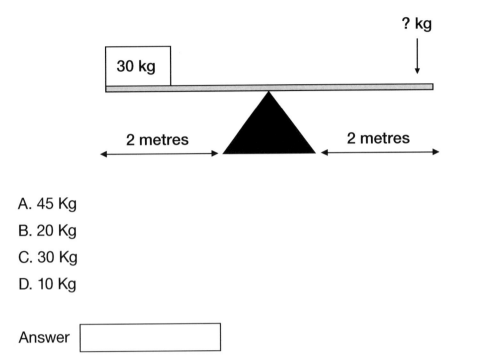

A. 45 Kg

B. 20 Kg

C. 30 Kg

D. 10 Kg

Answer [   ]

Question 9

How much weight in kilograms will need to be added in order to balance the beam?

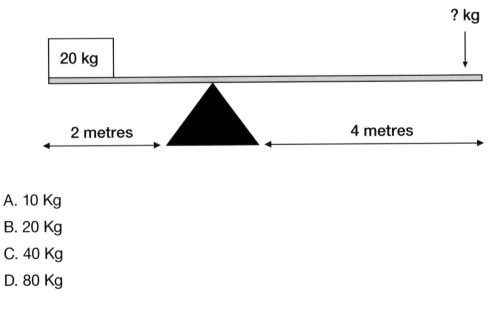

A. 10 Kg

B. 20 Kg

C. 40 Kg

D. 80 Kg

Answer [   ]

Question 10

How much weight in kilograms will need to be added in order to balance the beam?

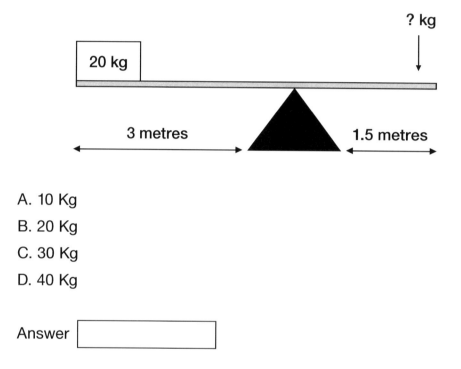

A. 10 Kg

B. 20 Kg

C. 30 Kg

D. 40 Kg

Answer [   ]

Question 11

Which crane is working under the least tension?

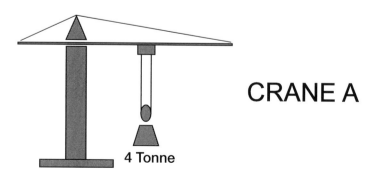

CRANE A

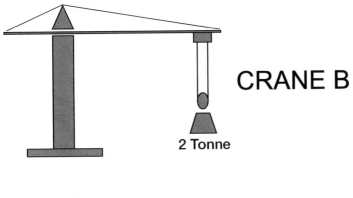

CRANE B

2 Tonne

A. Crane A

B. Crane B

C. Both the same

Answer

Question 12

Approximately how much force is required in order to lift the load?

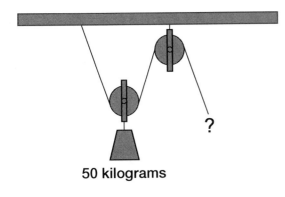

?

50 kilograms

A. 100 Kilograms

B. 50 kilograms

C. 25 Kilograms

D. 5 Kilograms

Answer [   ]

Question 13

If water is poured in at Point X, which tube will overflow first?

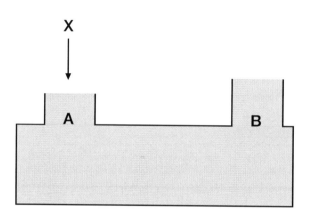

A. Tube A

B. Both at the same time

C. Tube B

Answer [   ]

Question 14

Which type of beam can take the greatest load?

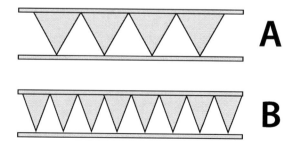

A. Beam A

B. Beam B

C. Both the same

Answer

Question 15

Which cog will make the most number of turns in 30 seconds?

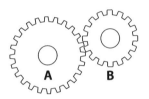

A. Cog A

B. Cog B

C. Both the same

Answer

Question 16

Which load is the heaviest?

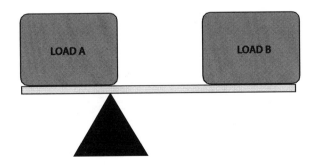

A. Load A

B. Load B

C. Both the same

Answer [   ]

Question 17

Which tank will not empty?

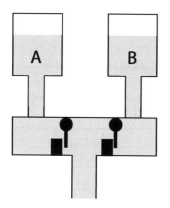

A. Tank A

B. Tank B

C. Both will not empty

Answer [   ]

Question 18

If cog Y moves anticlockwise which way will cog X move?

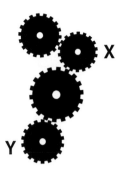

A. Anticlockwise

B. Clockwise

Answer

Question 19

How much weight is required to balance the load?

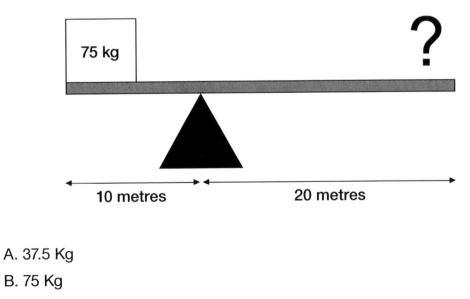

A. 37.5 Kg

B. 75 Kg

C. 125 Kg

D. 150 Kg

Answer [   ]

Question 20

At which point(s) should air enter the cylinder in order to force the piston downwards?

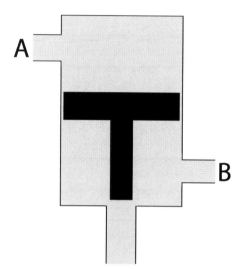

A. Point A

B. Points B

C. Points A and B

Answer [   ]

ANSWERS TO MECHANICAL COMPREHENSION TEST 2

1. A

Gate A is the strongest simply because there are more strengthening points in the construction of the gate and there are also three supporting hinges as opposed to two on gate B.

2. D

Only D has a mechanical advantage of 3 as it has three supporting ropes.

3. A

In order to take-off with the shortest runway the aircraft will require a head wind.

4. A

Wheel A is the largest and will therefore rotate the least number of times in any given time-frame.

5. A

Cog X will rotate anticlockwise.

6. A

Cog A will rotate 120 rpm clockwise. When answering questions of this nature it is advisable to count the number of teeth on each. In this particular scenario, each cog has the same number of teeth; therefore, the cogs will rotate at the same speed.

7. C

They will both hit the ground at the same time.

8. C

The distance of the weights from the fulcrum/balance point is identical; therefore, the weight required to balance the beam should be identical.

9. A

The distance of the weights from the fulcrum/balance pint is double; there-fore, the weight required to balance the beam should be halved.

10. D

The distance of the weights from the fulcrum/balance pint is halved; therefore, the weight required to balance the beam should be doubled.

11. C

They are both under the same tension. Although the weight lifted by crane A is double that of crane B, the weight is closer to the centre of gravity.

12. C

In this type of pulley system the mechanical advantage is 2; therefore, the effort required to lift the load is halved.

13. A

Point A is lower than point B will overflow first.

14. A

Beam A is the strongest because each triangular section covers a greater surface area.

15. B

The cog with the fewest teeth will make the most number of turns in any given time-frame. Because cog B has fewer teeth it will complete more turns that cog A.

16. A

Because the fulcrum/balance point is closer to load A this means that load B must be heavier in order to balance the beam. Therefore, load A is the heavier of the two.

17. B

Tank B will not empty because the valve will not permit water to flow past it.

18. A

19. A

The distance of the weights from the fulcrum/balance pint is double; therefore, the weight required to balance the beam should be halved.

20. A

CHAPTER 5

The Royal Navy Recruit Test – Numerical Reasoning Test Questions

ROYAL NAVY RECRUITING TEST NUMERICAL REASONING TEST - EXERCISE 1

During the Royal Navy Recruiting Test you will also be required to sit a numerical reasoning test. The test itself consists of 30 questions and you have 16 minutes to complete it. The most effective way to prepare for the test is to carry out plenty of practice in relation to addition, subtraction, multiplication, division and also fractions, percentages and algebra.

During the real test you won't normally be permitted to use a calculator but you will be provided with a blank sheet of paper so that you can work out your answers. Within this section I have provided you with lots of sample test questions to help you prepare. There are 30 questions in this test and you have 16 minutes in which to answer them. Use a blank sheet of paper to work out the answers.

ROYAL NAVY RECRUITING TEST NUMERICAL REASONING TEST EXERCISE 1

Question 1

$39 + ? = 64$

A. 25   B. 26   C. 28   D. 29   E. 30

Answer [   ]

Question 2

$111 - ? = 49$

A. 61   B. 62   C. 63   D. 64   E. 65

Answer [   ]

Question 3

$? + 337 = 622$

A. 280   B. 281   C. 282   D. 284   E. 285

Answer [   ]

Question 4

34 x ? = 272

A. 9   B. 8   C. 7   D. 6   E. 5

Answer [   ]

Question 5

22 + 11 + 19 = 13 x ?

A. 4   B. 3   C. 2   D. 4   E. 5

Answer [   ]

Question 6

(41 + 21) − 3 = ? + 45

A. 11   B. 12   C. 13   D.14   E. 15

Answer [   ]

Question 7

693 ÷ 99 = 5 + ?

A. 2   B. 4   C. 6   D. 7   E. 8

Answer [   ]

Question 8

291 - ? = 58 x 5

A. 1   B. 11   C. 21   D. 2   E. 22

Answer [   ]

Question 9

100 ÷ 4 = 97 - ?

A. 19   B. 73   C. 72   D. 69   E. 74

Answer [   ]

Question 10

41 x 2 = 103 ÷ ?

A. 19   B. 20   C. 21   D. 22   E. None of these

Answer [   ]

Question 11

Following the pattern shown in the number sequence below, what is the missing number?

6   18   ?   162   486   1458

A. 54   B. 48   C. 49   D. 101   E. 109

Answer [   ]

Question 12

If you count from 1 to 100, how many number 3s will you pass on the way?

A. 20   B. 19   C. 11   D. 12   E. 21

Answer [   ]

Question 13

50% of 448 = ?

A. 220   B. 226   C. 244   D. 224   E. 222

Answer [   ]

Question 14

25% of 6000 = ?

A. 1400   B. 1450   C. 1500   D. 1550   E. 1600

Answer [   ]

Question 15

20% of 200 = ?

A. 10   B. 15   C. 20   D. 30   E. 40

Answer [   ]

Question 16

20% of 250 = ?

A. 45   B. 35   C. 30   D. 15   E. 50

Answer [   ]

Question 17

45% of 1000 = ?

A. 4500   B. 450   C. 490   D. 500   E. 550

Answer

Question 18

14% of 300 = ?

A. 24   B. 34   C. 42   D. 160   E. 170

Answer

Question 19

1852 − 1582 = ?

A. 370   B. 375   C. 207   D. 270   E. 275

Answer

Question 20

8 x 5.5 = ?

A. 44   B. 42   C. 43   D. 48   E. 50

Answer

Question 21

888 ÷ 8 = ?

A. 422   B. 444   C. 222   D. 111   E. 224

Answer [   ]

Question 22

8383 − 383 = ?

A. 8097   B. 7808   C. 8000   D. 8003   E. 7999

Answer [   ]

Question 23

666 − (100 x 2) = ?

A. 566   B. 664   C. 466   D. 488   E. 566

Answer [   ]

Question 24

A rectangle has an area of 121cm². The length of one side is 11cm. What is the perimeter of the rectangle?

A. 44 inches   B. 44 cm   C. 242 cm   D. 242 inches   E. 110 cm

Answer [   ]

Question 25

A square has a perimeter of 32cm. What is the length of one side?

A. 8 cm   B. 128 cm   C. 18 cm   D. 8 metres   E. 9 cm

Answer [   ]

Question 26

During the Royal Navy Recruit Test a candidate achieves 45%. If the maximum possible score was 80, what score did the candidate achieve?

A. 45   B. 40   C. 46   D. 36   E. 50

Answer [   ]

Question 27

Is 1616 divisible by 16?

A. Yes   B. No

Answer [   ]

Question 28

During the Royal Navy Recruit Test a candidate achieves 40%. If the maximum possible score was 90, what score did the candidate achieve?

A. 34   B. 35   C. 36   D. 44   E. 45

Answer [   ]

Question 29

One side of a rectangle is 30 cm. If the area of the rectangle is 570 cm², what is the length of the other side?

A. 15cm   B. 17 cm   C. 6 cm   D. 7 cm   E. 19 cm

Answer [   ]

Question 30

A rectangle has an area of 144cm². The length of one side is 16cm. What is the perimeter?

A. 8cm   B. 16cm   C. 10cm   D. 12cm   E. None of these.

Answer [   ]

Now that you have completed the first numerical reasoning exercise, take the time to check through your answers carefully before moving onto exercise 2.

ANSWERS TO NUMERICAL REASONING EXERCISE 1

1. A
2. B
3. E
4. B
5. D
6. D
7. A
8. A
9. C
10. E
11. A
12. A
13. D
14. C
15. E
16. E
17. B
18. C
19. D
20. A

21. D

22. C

23. C

24. B

25. A

26. D

27. A

28. C

29. E

30. E

ROYAL NAVY RECRUITING TEST NUMERICAL REASONING TEST - EXERCISE 2

There are 30 questions in this exercise and you have 16 minutes in which to answer them. Once again use a blank sheet of paper to work out the answers. You are not permitted to use a calculator.

Question 1

Subtract 6.99 from 18.09

A.	B.	C.	D.	E.
1	10.11	10.01	11.1	11.01

Answer [   ]

Question 2

What is 0.5 expressed as a fraction?

A.	B.	C.	D.	E.
½	¼	5.0	0.25	1.5

Answer

Question 3

What is 47.889097 correct to three significant figures

A.	B.	C.	D.	E.
49	48.1	47.9	47.8	488

Answer

Question 4

What is 69.969097 correct to three significant figures

A.	B.	C.	D.	E.
71.0	69	69.6	69.9	70

Answer

Question 5

Steven scores 70% in a test. If the maximum score was 90, what score did he achieve?

A.	B.	C.	D.	E.
63	64	65	80	73

Answer

Question 6

Subtract 9.8 from 21.1

A.	B.	C.	D.	E.
11.3	10.3	9.9	11.7	11.4

Answer [   ]

Question 7

Calculate 44 x 22

A.	B.	C.	D.	E.
444	888	968	986	880

Answer [   ]

Question 8

If x = 151 and y = 11, then x minus y = ?

A.	B.	C.	D.	E.
150	145	141	140	141

Answer [   ]

Question 9

Calculate 21.1 x 3

A.	B.	C.	D.	E.
33	33.1	33.3	61.3	63.3

Answer [   ]

Question 10

If x = 111 and y = 27, then x minus y = ?

A.	B.	C.	D.	E.
88	85	86	184	84

Answer [   ]

Question 11

Convert 0.75 to a fraction?

A. 1/75   B. 3/4   C. 7/5   D. 2/5   E. 4/6

Answer [   ]

Question 12

John wants to lose 16 kilograms in weight. After 4 months he has lost ¾ of this amount. How much has lost?

A. 5 kg   B. 4 kg   C. 7 kg   D. 12 kg   E. 8 kg

Answer [   ]

Question 13

Calculate 3/5 - 1/5

A. 4/5   B. 2/5   C. 1/2   D. 1/4   E. 3/5

Answer [   ]

Question 14

If r = 41 and s = 966, then s – y =

A. 295   B. 95   C. 930   D. 935   E. 925

Answer [   ]

Question 15

25 out of 80 hospital patients have arm injuries. What percentage of patients do not have arm injuries?

A. 68.75%   B. 66%   C. 69.37%   D. 70%   E. 65.85%"

Answer [   ]

Question 16

Alison has been keeping a record of how much she has been withdrawing from the cash point machine. Over the last 8 weeks she has withdrawn the following amounts:

£10   £25   £60   £60   £20   £10   £90   £100

What percentage of her withdrawals are under £60?

A. 40%   B. 50%   C. 60%   D. 70%   E. 65%

Answer [   ]

Question 17

Calculate: 3/8 ÷ 3/4

A. 1/2   B. 2/25   C. 3/4   D. 1/8   E. 2/32

Answer [   ]

Question 18

45 out of 120 hospital patients have leg injuries. What percentage of patients have leg injuries?

A. 35.75%   B. 45%   C. 37.5%   D. 30%   E. 25.5%"

Answer [   ]

Question 19

12 out of 120 hospital patients have neck injuries. What percentage of patients do not have neck injuries?

A. 10   B. 54   C. 12   D. 80   E. 90

Answer [   ]

Question 20

What is the number 42.87244 correct to three decimal places?

A. 42.9   B. 43.0   C. 44.0   D. 42.8   E. 43.87

Answer [   ]

Question 21

The clock below reads 3pm. How many degrees will the small (hour) hand have turned when the time reaches 9pm?

A. 180°   B. 90°   C. 360°   D. 60°   E. 30°

Answer [   ]

Question 22

The clock below reads 3pm. How many degrees will the large (minute) hand have turned when the time reaches 4pm?

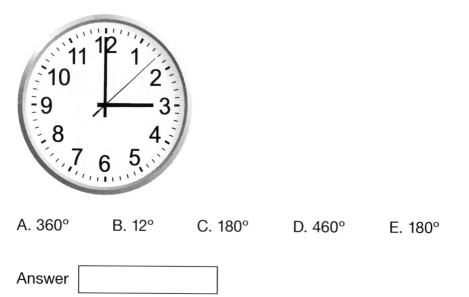

A. 360°   B. 12°   C. 180°   D. 460°   E. 180°

Answer [   ]

Question 23

The clock below reads 3pm. How many degrees will the large (minute) hand have turned when the time reaches 4:45pm?

A. 105°   B. 270°   C. 320°   D. 405°   E. 630°

Answer [   ]

Question 24

The clock below reads 3pm. How many degrees will the small (hour) hand have turned when the time reaches 8pm?

A. 1440°   B. 150°   C. 50°   D. 300°   E. 270°

Answer [   ]

Question 25

The clock below reads 3pm. How many degrees will the small (hour) hand have turned when the time reaches 11pm?

A. 45°   B. 8°   C. 240°   D. 80°   E. 270°

Answer [   ]

Question 26

The clock below reads 3am. How many degrees will the large (hour) hand have turned when the time reaches 3pm?

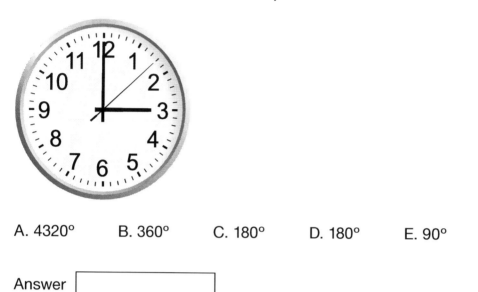

A. 4320°   B. 360°   C. 180°   D. 180°   E. 90°

Answer [   ]

Question 27

The Fire Service reports the following number and type of fires in a 12 month period:

Car fires	100
Chimney fires	200
House fires	50
Derelict building fires	300
Rubbish fires	350

What percentage of fires were car fires?

A. 10%   B. 15%   C. 20%   D. 25%   E. 30%

Answer [   ]

Question 28

The Fire Service reports the following number and type of fires in a 12 month period:

Car fires	200
Chimney fires	100
House fires	350
Derelict building fires	150
Rubbish fires	200

What percentage of fires were house fires?

A. 10%   B. 350%   C. 20%   D. 35%   E. 30%

Answer [   ]

Question 29

1300 x 0.6 = ?

A. 7,800   B. 78   C. 990   D. 780   E. 870

Answer [   ]

Question 30

770 x 0.1 = ?

A. 77   B. 7.7   C. 770   D. 770.01   E. 770.1

Answer [   ]

Now that you have completed numerical reasoning exercise 2 take the time to carefully work through your answers before onto the final section of the guide.

ANSWERS TO NUMERICAL REASONING TEST EXERCISE 2

1. D
2. A
3. C
4. E
5. A
6. A
7. C
8. D
9. E
10. E
11. B
12. D
13. B
14. E
15. A
16. B
17. A
18. C
19. E
20. A
21. A
22. A
23. E

24. B

25. C

26. A

27. A

28. D

29. D

30. A

You have now reached the end of the testing guide and I am sure you will have found the questions useful in your preparation for taking the Royal Navy test. If you would like further test questions, I have another book available on Amazon, entitled ARMED FORCES TESTS. Simply go to Amazon and search for **'Richard McMunn Armed Forces Tests'** to locate the book.

Good luck with your test!

Richard McMunn

OVERCOMING TEST NERVES

The majority of people who are required to undertake any form of test will get nervous. This is only natural and without some degree of nerves you won't be able to perform to the best of your ability. However, some people will unfortunately experience uncontrollable nerves. It is only natural to feel nervous before a test but there are a number of things that you can do to get over these nerves. To begin with, lets take a look at a few of the more common pre-test anxieties:

- Feeling generally nervous and anxious
- Sweaty hands and palms
- Trembling voice
- Sore head
- Aching muscles
- Dry mouth
- Increased heart beat
- Shaky hands

I can remember taking my driving test at the age of 17 and feeling a few of the above symptoms. In the build up to the test I had worried myself so much that eventually I thought, "What's the point in all of this? It's only a driving test, who cares if I fail?" I had seriously reached the point where I didn't really care anymore whether I passed or failed. Now this is probably going to sound stupid, but this change in attitude actually worked in my favour. I performed a lot better during the driving test, simply because inside I had stopped caring, and therefore the nerves went out of the window. Now I am not saying that you shouldn't care about your tests, because that would be silly. But what I am saying is that you can only do so much practice and you can only do so many mock tests. Once you have done sufficient preparation for the tests, and you will know when that time has come, then it is pointless worrying anymore about it. Do your study, do your preparation, and then go to the test centre feeling free, calm and relaxed, and trust me, you will perform a whole lot better!

Visualising the test before you attend it

This is a great method that works for many people. Before you attend the test, try and visualise the entire process. Sit down in your favourite armchair and close your eyes. Think about driving to the test centre with plenty of time to spare. You arrive early at the venue and sit in the car park composing yourself and reading through a number of sample test questions. When you walk into the test centre you are standing tall, smiling and feeling relaxed and confident. You introduce yourself in a polite manner and shake the hands of the assessor. You sit down in the chair and listen carefully to all instructions. Once the test commences you work quickly, yet calmly, and you try your hardest to answer all of the questions accurately. Once you have completed the test you take the time to go back through your answers.

The above method is a fantastic way of focusing yourself prior to any test. If you try to visualise the entire process being successful before the event starts, then this will put you in the correct frame of mind.

Alternative testing resources

I hope that you have found this guide to be a great use in your preparation for the Armed Forces tests. You can also obtain further testing resources from the website www.how2become.com including sample online testing questions.

how2become

Visit www.how2become.com to find more titles and courses that will help you to pass any job interview or selection process:

- Online Armed forces test questions
- Royal Navy DVDs and books
- 1-day intensive career training courses
- Psychometric testing books and CDs

www.How2Become.com

20618832R00060

Printed in Poland
by Amazon Fulfillment
Poland Sp. z o.o., Wrocław